THIS IS A WELBECK CHILDREN'S BOOK
Published in 2022 by Welbeck Children's Books Limited
An imprint of the Welbeck Publishing Group
Based in London and Sydney
www.welbeckpublishing.com
Text © 2022 Simon Mugford
Design & Illustration © 2022 Dan Green
ISBN: 978-1-78312-760-3

Writer: Simon Mugford
Designer and Illustrator: Dan Green
Design manager: Sam James
Commissioning editor: Suhel Ahmed
Production: Arlene Alexander

A catalogue record for this book is available from the British Library.

Printed in the UK
10 9 8 7 6 5 4 3 2 1

Statistics and records correct as of January 2022

SPORTS SUPERSTARS

HAMILTON RULES

SIMON MUGFORD   DAN GREEN

CONTENTS

CHAPTER 1

RACING KING

HAMILTON RULES

Racing driver **Sir Lewis Hamilton** is a

GLOBAL SPORTS SUPERSTAR.

Seven-times winner of the World Drivers' Championship, Hamilton has broken **multiple records** and blazed a trail as the **first *BLACK* driver** in *Formula One.*

THIS BOOK IS ALL ABOUT **HIM!**

7

WHAT MAKES HAMILTON SUCH AN *AWESOME* DRIVER?

AGGRESSION

Lewis has an attacking style on the track. He is one of the sport's best overtakers with a winning mentality.

TECHNICAL

He works closely with his race engineers and knows his car's tyres, brakes, steering - everything - inside out.

ZOOM!

44

SPEED
Forget the technical stuff, Hamilton is just flat-out fast, even in the wet.

TACTICAL
Lewis makes the right decisions and times them perfectly to beat his opponents.

WINNING
Finishing first is what Lewis does best - over and over again.

He's *wheely* great!

GROAN.

LEWIS IN NUMBERS

Hamilton's **FORMULA ONE** stats are **OFF THE SCALE!**

7 WORLD CHAMPIONSHIP WINS
(A record, shared with Michael Schumacher)

182 PODIUM FINISHES
(the most)

103 POLE POSITIONS
(the most)

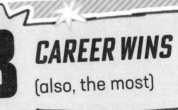
103 CAREER WINS
(also, the most)

More than

4,000

WORLD CHAMPIONSHIP POINTS

(yep, more than anyone else)

Estimated

£225

MILLION fortune

26.7 MILLION

Instagram followers

HAMILTON I.D.

NAME: Lewis Carl Davidson Hamilton

DATE OF BIRTH: 7 January 1985

PLACE OF BIRTH: Stevenage, England

NATIONALITY: British

TEAMS: McLaren (2007-2012), Mercedes (2013-present)

CAR NUMBER: 44

NICKNAME: Billion Dollar Man

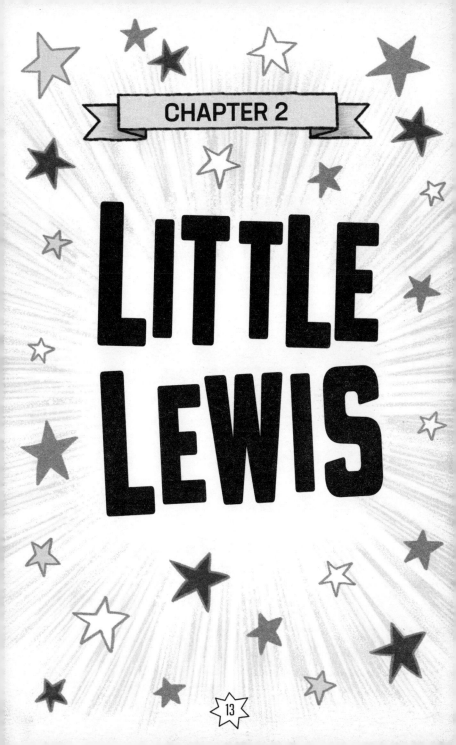

CHAPTER 2

LITTLE LEWIS

Lewis Hamilton was born in a town called **Stevenage** in England, in **1985.**

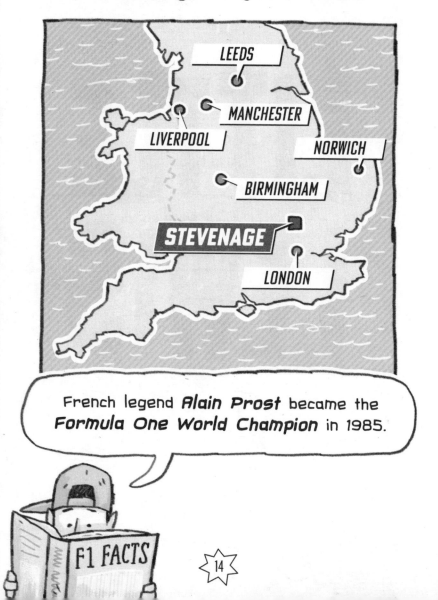

LEEDS

MANCHESTER

LIVERPOOL

NORWICH

BIRMINGHAM

STEVENAGE

LONDON

French legend **Alain Prost** became the **Formula One World Champion** in 1985.

F1 FACTS

There was his Dad,

Anthony . . .

And his Mum, **Carmen.**

Lewis's mum and dad
separated when he was two.

Lewis' half-brother
Nicolas is also a
racing driver.

For his **FIFTH** birthday, Lewis was given a **radio-controlled car.** It was the start of his love of racing cars.

Young Lewis raced radio-controlled cars against grown-ups - and he usually **won!**

He even appeared on children's **television** to show off his **skills.**

Lewis **LOVED** racing cars so much, his dad bought him **racing go-kart** for Christmas.

To Lewis
Merry Xmas
Love Dad x

It was an old go-kart and his dad

spent **A LOT** of time fixing it up.

In **1993**, when Lewis was **eight**, he started racing at his local track, the **Rye House Kart Raceway.**

Go-kart racing is **VERY** expensive. The Hamilton family were not rich, so Lewis's dad worked **VERY** hard so his son could race.

YAWN

RRRMMMM

"MY DAD TOLD ME WHEN I WAS SIX OR SEVEN YEARS OLD NEVER TO GIVE UP AND THAT'S KIND OF THE FAMILY MOTTO."

Lewis Hamilton.

CHAPTER 3

KARTING KID

Lewis **stood out** from all the other kids at the races. He and his dad would turn up in an **old car** with their **old go-kart . . .**

And he was the **only** black kid at the race track.

BUT . . .

Lewis was fast, **brilliant** at overtaking and handled the kart like no-one else could.

He soon won race after race after race. . .

In **1995,** when he was TEN, Lewis won the **BRITISH SUPER ONE KART CHAMPIONSHIPS.**

YOUNGEST EVER WINNER

At the **Autosport Awards** that year, Lewis asked the **McLaren F1 team** boss **Ron Dennis** for an autograph.

By **1998** Lewis had won another British Championship and Ron Dennis **CALLED HIM.**

McLaren offered to help Lewis become a **Formula One driver.** It was an unbelievable offer. His family would not have to pay for his racing any more.

But Lewis had to **promise** to work hard at school!

GO KART BREAKDOWN

Go-kart racing began in the *USA* in the *1950s*. The early karts used petrol engines from *lawnmowers* or *chainsaws!*

ALLOY TUBE CHASSIS

At 15, Lewis was racing in **Formula A** (the highest class of karting) with team-mate **Nico Rosberg.**

The two boys competed on the track, then tried to beat each other at everything from **table tennis** and **video games** to **eating pizza** and **unicycling!**

In 2000, Lewis won the **Formula A European Championship.**

HAMILTON'S BIG KARTING WINS

SEASON	SERIES	CLASS
1995	SUPER 1 NATIONAL CHAMPIONSHIP	IAME CADET
1996	KARTMASTERS BRITISH GRAND PRIX	COMER CADET
1997	SUPER 1 NATIONAL CHAMPIONSHIP	FORMULA YAMAHA
1999	TORNEO INDUSTRIE OPEN	ICA
2000	WORLD CUP	FORMULA A
2000	EUROPEAN CHAMPIONSHIP	FORMULA A

CHAPTER 4

MAGIC FORMULA

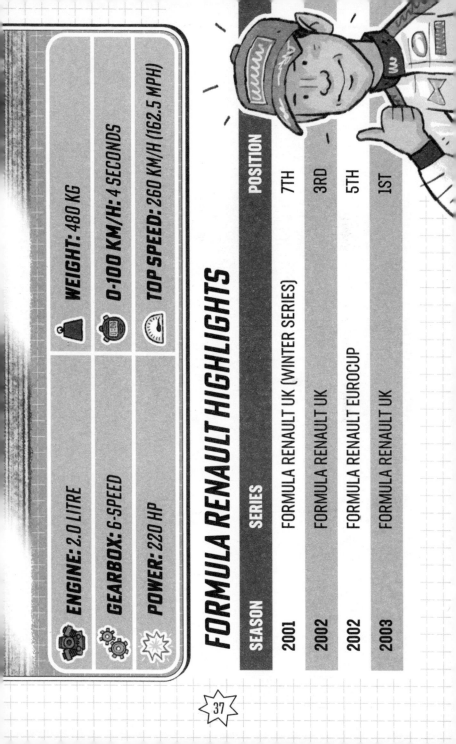

ENGINE: 2.0 LITRE

WEIGHT: 480 KG

GEARBOX: 6-SPEED

0-100 KM/H: 4 SECONDS

POWER: 220 HP

TOP SPEED: 260 KM/H (162.5 MPH)

FORMULA RENAULT HIGHLIGHTS

SEASON	SERIES	POSITION
2001	FORMULA RENAULT UK (WINTER SERIES)	7TH
2002	FORMULA RENAULT UK	3RD
2002	FORMULA RENAULT EUROCUP	5TH
2003	FORMULA RENAULT UK	1ST

ENGINE: 3.4 LITRE

GEARBOX: 6-SPEED

POWER: 380 HP

WEIGHT: 550 KG

0-100 KM/H: 3.1 SECONDS

TOP SPEED: 300 KM/H (186 MPH)

FORMULA 3 HIGHLIGHTS

SEASON	SERIES	POSITION
2004	FORMULA 3 EURO SERIES	5TH
2004	BAHRAIN SUPERPRIX	1ST
2005	FORMULA 3 EURO SERIES	1ST
2005	MASTERS OF FORMULA 3	1ST

GP2

GP2 (now known as Formula 2) is the next step for a driver aiming to race in F1.

VVAROOM!

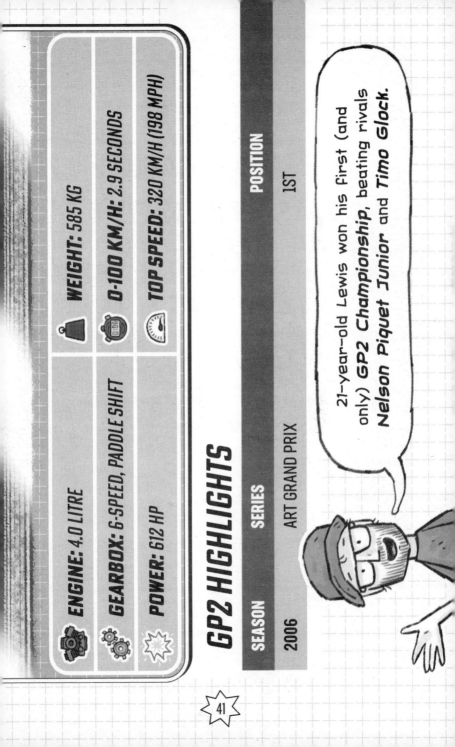

ENGINE: 4.0 LITRE

WEIGHT: 585 KG

GEARBOX: 6-SPEED, PADDLE SHIFT

0-100 KM/H: 2.9 SECONDS

POWER: 612 HP

TOP SPEED: 320 KM/H (198 MPH)

GP2 HIGHLIGHTS

SEASON	SERIES	POSITION
2006	ART GRAND PRIX	1ST

21-year-old Lewis won his first (and only) *GP2 Championship*, beating rivals *Nelson Piquet Junior* and *Timo Glock*.

"LEWIS'S PERFORMANCE WAS THE MOST PHENOMENAL I HAVE SEEN IN A GP2 RACE."

McLaren boss Martin Whitmarsh on Hamilton's GP2 win at the Nürburgring in 2006.

CHAPTER 5

F1
FANTASTIC

In **2007**, a place WAS available in the

McLaren Formula One team and . . .

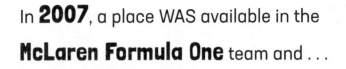

HAMILTON BECAME AN *F1 DRIVER*.

Lewis was **22** years old.

The other McLaren driver was the defending
World Champion, **Fernando Alonso.** The
team-mates would soon became **BIG** rivals.

RECORD ROOKIE

Hamilton finished **THIRD** in his first F1 race
- the **2007 Australian Grand Prix**.

It kicked off a record-breaking season for

the rookie driver . . .

MOST **WINS** IN A DEBUT SEASON **4**

MOST **POLE POSITIONS** IN A DEBUT SEASON **6**

MOST **POINTS** IN A DEBUT SEASON **109**

YOUNGEST DRIVER TO LEAD THE WORLD CHAMPIONSHIP

22 YEARS, 126 DAYS

His first win was the **Canadian Grand Prix** on **10 June 2007**.

Lewis finished **SECOND** in the Championship, behind Ferrari's **Kimi Räikkönen** and just ahead of his rival **Alonso.**

HUMPF!

2008

AN INCREDIBLE YEAR

Hamilton's incredible first season had made him **WORLD FAMOUS.** As the first ever black F1 driver, Lewis was making sporting history.

Lewis began the **2008 season** in style - taking **POLE POSITION** and **WINNING** the Australian Grand Prix.

But he also made **mistakes**, and took **risks**, but not all of them were successful.

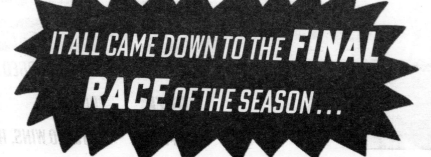

IT ALL CAME DOWN TO THE *FINAL RACE* OF THE SEASON...

Hamilton was leading the Championship, with Ferrari driver **Felipe Massa** (on his home circuit) in second place.

If Lewis finished **FIFTH** or better, he would be champion . . .

Lewis was careful not to take chances and as the rain came down, he was in **SIXTH** . . . until he overtook Timo Glock at the **FINAL CORNER** of the **LAST** lap . . .

Massa won the race and the home crowd were wildly celebrating a Brazilian win . . . until they realized that actually, Lewis had **won the Championship** by a **SINGLE POINT!**

HAMILTON WAS AN INTERNATIONAL SENSATION.

HE WAS THE **YOUNGEST F1 CHAMPIONSHIP WINNER** (23 YEARS, 301 DAYS)

Sebastian Vettel became the youngest in **2010**.

LEWIS WAS THE FIRST **BRITISH WORLD CHAMPION** SINCE **DAMON HILL** IN 1996.

AND IMPORTANTLY, LEWIS WAS THE FIRST (AND IS STILL THE ONLY) **BLACK F1 CHAMPION.**

HAMILTON'S RECORD AT MCLAREN

SEASON	RACES	WINS	POLES	PODIUMS	POINTS	POSITION
2007	17	4	6	12	109	2nd
2008	18	5	7	10	98	1st
2009	17	2	4	5	49	5th
2010	19	3	1	9	240	4th
2011	19	3	1	6	227	5th
2012	20	4	7	7	190	4th

CHAPTER 6

TOP TRACKS

HUNGARY

NAME: HUNGARORING

GRAND PRIX: HUNGARIAN

LOCATION: MOGYORÓD, HUNGARY

LENGTH: 4.381 KM

TURNS: 14

RACE LAP RECORD: 1:16.627 *(Lewis Hamilton, 2020)*

HAMILTON IN HUNGARY

POLE POSITIONS:	EIGHT
PODIUM FINISHES:	TEN
WINS:	EIGHT

Lewis has won **EIGHT TIMES** in Hungary — more times than at any other circuit.

BRAZIL

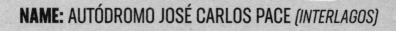

NAME: AUTÓDROMO JOSÉ CARLOS PACE *(INTERLAGOS)*

GRAND PRIX: BRAZILIAN

LOCATION: SÃO PAULO, BRAZIL

LENGTH: 4.309 KM

TURNS: 15

RACE LAP RECORD: 1:10.540 *(Valtteri Bottas, 2018)*

HAMILTON IN BRAZIL

POLE POSITIONS:	THREE
PODIUM FINISHES:	FIVE
WINS:	TWO

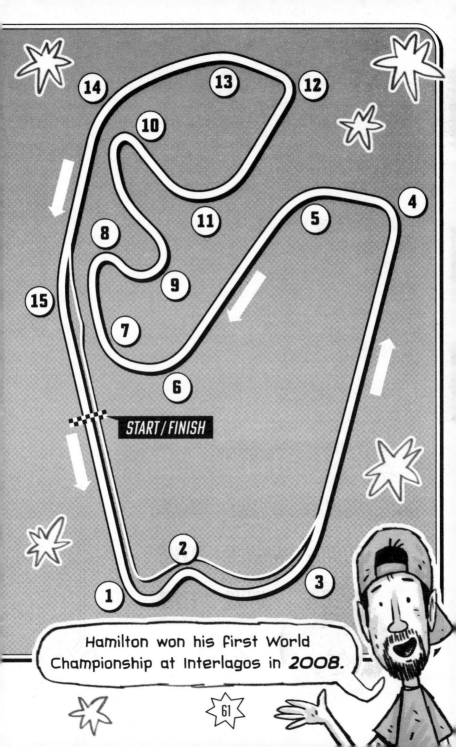

START / FINISH

Hamilton won his first World Championship at Interlagos in *2008.*

MONACO

NAME: CIRCUIT DE MONACO

GRAND PRIX: MONACO

LOCATION: MONTE CARLO, MONACO

LENGTH: 3.337 KM

TURNS: 19

RACE LAP RECORD: 1:12.909 *(Lewis Hamilton, 2021)*

HAMILTON AT MONACO

POLE POSITIONS:	**TWO**
PODIUM FINISHES:	**SEVEN**
WINS:	**THREE**

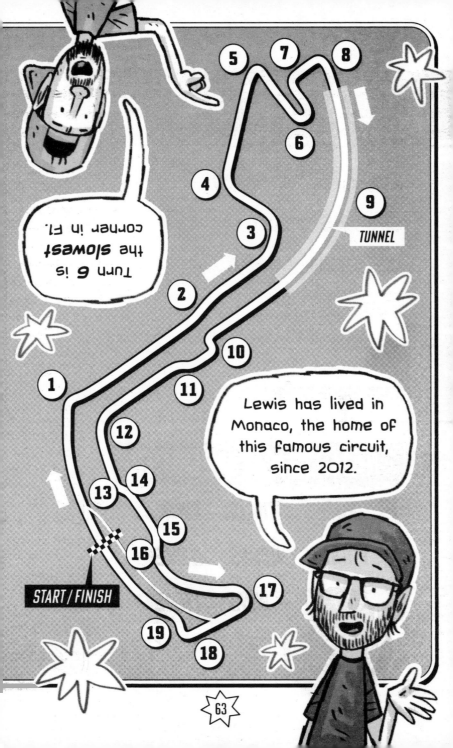

SILVERSTONE

NAME: SILVERSTONE CIRCUIT

GRAND PRIX: BRITISH

LOCATION: SILVERSTONE, UK

LENGTH: 5.891 KM

TURNS: 18

RACE LAP RECORD: 1:27.097 *(Max Verstappen, 2020)*

HAMILTON AT SILVERSTONE

POLE POSITIONS:	**SEVEN**
PODIUM FINISHES:	**TWELVE**
WINS:	**EIGHT**

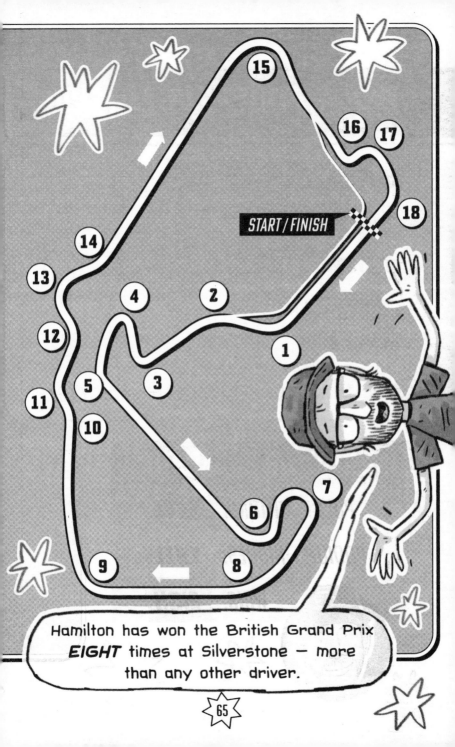

Hamilton has won the British Grand Prix **EIGHT** times at Silverstone — more than any other driver.

CIRCUIT GILLES VILLENEUVE

NAME: CIRCUIT GILLES VILLENEUVE

GRAND PRIX: CANADIAN

LOCATION: MONTREAL, CANADA

LENGTH: 4.361 KM

TURNS: 13

RACE LAP RECORD: 1:13.078 *(Valtteri Bottas, 2019)*

HAMILTON IN CANADA

POLE POSITIONS:	*SIX*
PODIUM FINISHES:	*EIGHT*
WINS:	*SEVEN*

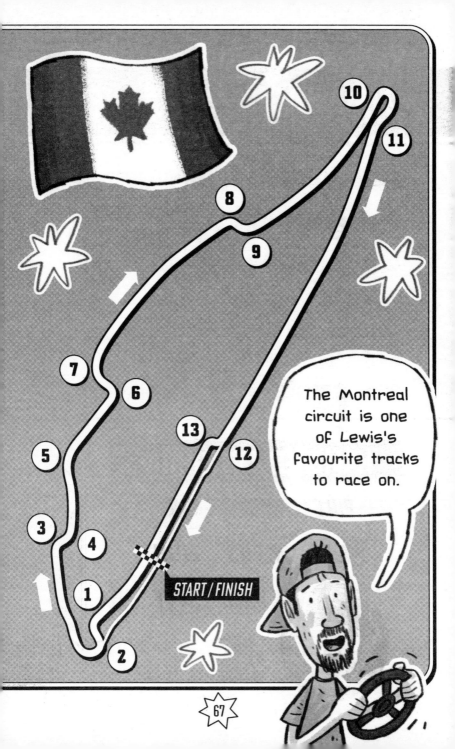

The Montreal circuit is one of Lewis's favourite tracks to race on.

START / FINISH

CHINA

NAME: SHANGHAI INTERNATIONAL CIRCUIT

GRAND PRIX: CHINESE

LOCATION: SHANGHAI, CHINA

LENGTH: 5.451 KM

TURNS: 16

RACE LAP RECORD: 1:32.238 *(Michael Schumacher, 2004)*

HAMILTON IN CHINA

POLE POSITIONS:	*SIX*
PODIUM FINISHES:	*NINE*
WINS:	*SIX*

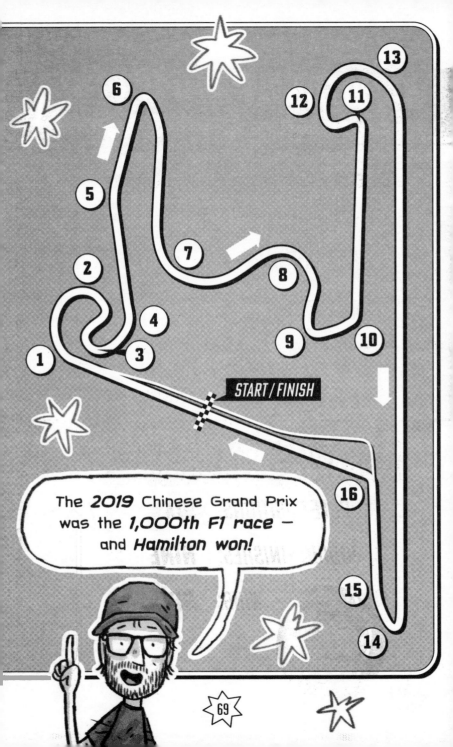

HAMILTON'S WINNING GPs

TRACK	WINS
HUNGARY	8
GREAT BRITAIN	8
CANADA	7
SPAIN	6
SHANGHAI	6
ABU DHABI	5
BAHRAIN	5
ITALY	5
USA	5
RUSSIA	5

CHAPTER 7

MERCEDES MAGIC

Lewis failed to win another Championship with **McLaren**, but he surprised most F1 fans with a move to **Mercedes** in **2013.**

"IT IS NOW TIME FOR ME TO TAKE ON A FRESH CHALLENGE AND I AM VERY EXCITED TO BEGIN A NEW CHAPTER."

Hamilton was reunited with his old karting (and pizza-eating) friend and rival **Nico Rosberg.**

It was the start of an **AWESOME** era for Lewis and the team known as The **Silver Arrows.**

2014

CHAMPION AGAIN!

This season was all about **Hamilton** versus **Rosberg.** The Mercedes duo took **first** or **second** place in **11 races.**

It all came down to the final race – the **Abu Dhabi Grand Prix.** Rosberg started on pole, but ... it was **Lewis** who finished first.

Hamilton was F1 World Champion for the

SECOND TIME.

▰▰▰▰	POLES	FASTEST LAPS	WINS	POINTS
HAMILTON	7	7	11	384
ROSBERG	11	5	5	317

2015

SEASON HIGHLIGHTS

15 MARCH 2015
AUSTRALIAN GRAND PRIX

Lewis began the defence of his title in pole position – and **finished first!** Rosberg was a close second with third-placed **Sebastian Vettel** more than 30 seconds behind.

24 MAY 2015
MONACO GRAND PRIX

Lewis started on **pole** for the first time on the famous street circuit. But after a pitstop mistake, Hamilton finished **third,** behind Vettel and a **victorious Rosberg.**

25 OCTOBER 2015
UNITED STATES GRAND PRIX

In an eventful race in wet conditions, Hamilton and Rosberg battled it out for first and second, with Lewis the eventual winner. Rosberg was not happy!

Hamilton was champion for a **THIRD** time – the same as his idol **Ayrton Senna**.

	POLES	FASTEST LAPS	WINS	POINTS
HAMILTON	*11*	*8*	*10*	*381*
ROSBERG	*7*	*5*	*6*	*322*

FOUR MORE

In **2016,** Rosberg got his revenge as he beat Lewis to the Championship by just **FIVE POINTS.**

Then Rosberg **retired** from F1!

Over the next **four seasons,** Hamilton fought off challenges from . . .

Sebastian Vettel . . .

Valtteri Bottas . . .

Lewis's new team-mate

and a young Dutch driver called **Max Verstappen . . .**

to win an **UNBELIEVABLE** four Championships in a row. The **2020** win was his **SEVENTH** – equalling the record held by **Michael Schumacher.**

LEWIS'S WINNING CARS

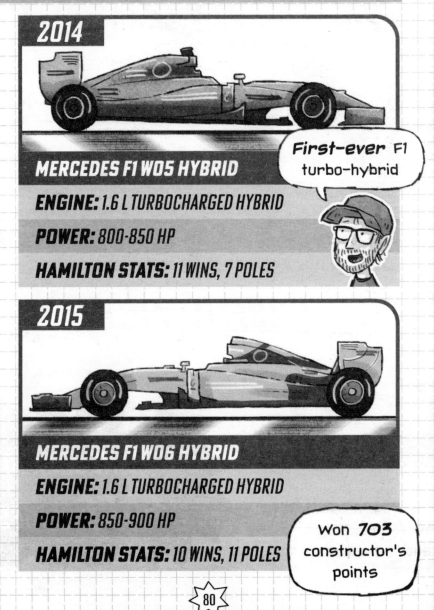

2014

MERCEDES F1 W05 HYBRID

ENGINE: 1.6 L TURBOCHARGED HYBRID

POWER: 800-850 HP

HAMILTON STATS: 11 WINS, 7 POLES

First-ever F1 turbo-hybrid

2015

MERCEDES F1 W06 HYBRID

ENGINE: 1.6 L TURBOCHARGED HYBRID

POWER: 850-900 HP

HAMILTON STATS: 10 WINS, 11 POLES

Won **703** constructor's points

2017

Lewis recorded **seven** fastest laps in this car.

MERCEDES AMG F1 WO8 EQ POWER+

ENGINE: 1.6 L TURBOCHARGED HYBRID

POWER: 950-1000 HP

HAMILTON STATS: 9 WINS, 11 POLES

2018

Lewis scored over **400** points in this car.

MERCEDES AMG F1 WO9 EQ POWER+

ENGINE: 1.6 L TURBOCHARGED HYBRID

POWER: 950-1000 HP

HAMILTON STATS: 11 WINS, 11 POLES

2019

Won Mercedes a *sixth* constructor's title in a row

MERCEDES AMG F1 W10 EQ POWER+

ENGINE: 1.6 L TURBOCHARGED HYBRID

POWER: 950-1000 HP

HAMILTON STATS: 11 WINS, 5 POLES

2020

The most *powerful* Mercedes F1 car so far

MERCEDES-AMG F1 W11 EQ PERFORMANCE

ENGINE: 1.6 L TURBOCHARGED HYBRID

POWER: 1025 HP

HAMILTON STATS: 11 WINS, 10 POLES

F1 FACTS

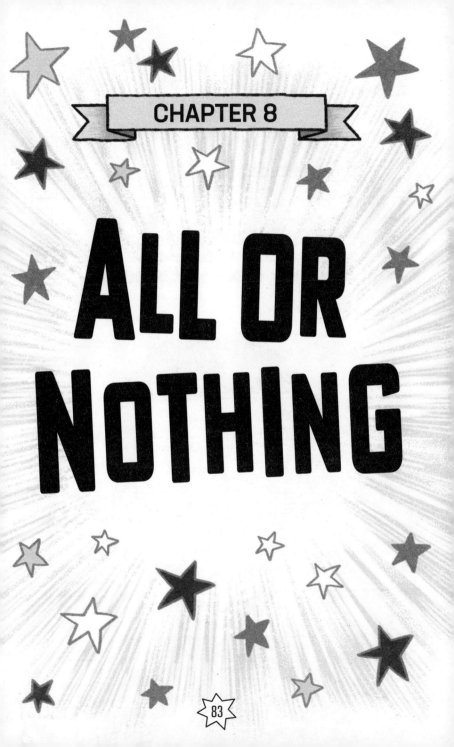

CHAPTER 8

ALL OR NOTHING

2021 was the season where Hamilton could win a record-breaking **EIGHTH World Championship.**

But Hamilton's newest rival, the young **Red Bull** driver, **Max Verstappen** had other ideas.

It was a season full of **crazy** scenes, **crashes** and intense **competition**.

OOOF!

Lewis

They had a **spectacular** clash at the **Italian** Grand Prix.

"MAD MAX" PUSHED LEWIS TO THE LIMIT.

5 DECEMBER 2021

SAUDI ARABIAN GRAND PRIX

Verstappen led Hamilton by **EIGHT points** before this race - the first ever **Saudi Arabian Grand Prix.**

The race was **CRAZY!**

LET'S DO THIS!

Verstappen was penalised and told to **drop back a place**. He **braked suddenly** and Lewis ran into the back of him!

Max let Lewis past, but then sped up again!

Hamilton eventually won what was the most dramatic and eventful Grand Prix for many years!

HUMPF!

12 DECEMBER 2021

ABU DHABI GRAND PRIX

The two rivals were **level on points.** It would be **winner takes all.**

Hamilton started behind Verstappen in **second place** . . . but he took the lead on the first lap and kept it for almost the entire race!

But after a safety car and a strange decision that took **SOME** lapped cars out of the race, Verstappen, with fresh tyres, overtook Lewis on the **final lap.**

And that was it. Verstappen was the

WORLD CHAMPION.

Lewis and the Mercedes team could not believe it.

After the race, Lewis proved to be a true **sports star.** He congratulated Verstappen and said,

"I'M SO PROUD OF MY OWN TEAM AND WE GAVE IT ABSOLUTELY EVERYTHING . . . WE'LL SEE WHAT HAPPENS NEXT YEAR."

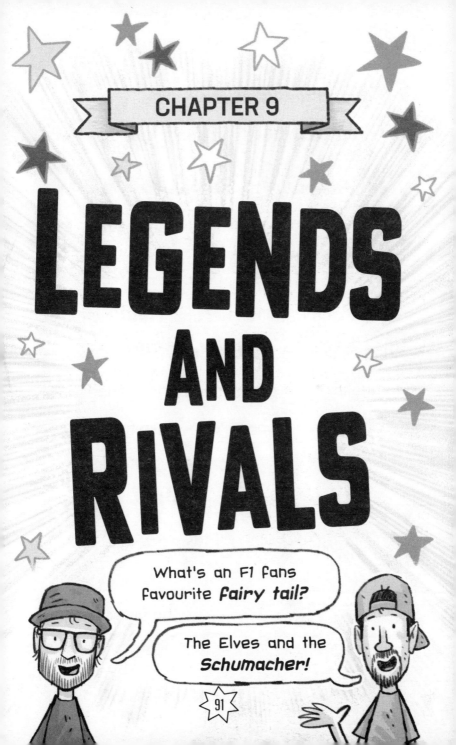

RIVAL

NAME: **FERNANDO ALONSO**

YEARS IN F1: **2001-**

TEAMS: **MINARDI, RENAULT, McLAREN, FERRARI, ALPINE**

CHAMPIONSHIP WINS: **TWO**

Alonso and Hamilton became **rivals** when they both joined **McLaren** in **2007.**

In qualifying at that season's Hungarian Grand Prix, Alonso famously **blocked** Lewis in the pit lane. **BUT** . . . Alonso has since said that Hamilton is "one of the top five drivers in F1 history".

LEGEND

NAME: **AYRTON SENNA**

YEARS IN F1: **1984-1994**

TEAMS: **TOLEMAN, LOTUS, McLAREN, WILLIAMS**

CHAMPIONSHIP WINS: **THREE**

Senna was Hamilton's idol - as he was to millions of race fans around the world. Senna's rivalry with **Alain Prost** is the stuff of **F1 legend** and both race fans and the wider world were shocked after his death in a crash at the 1994 San Marino Grand Prix.

RIVAL

NAME: SEBASTIAN VETTEL

YEARS IN F1: 2007-

TEAMS: BMW SAUBER, TORO ROSSO, RED BULL, FERRARI, ASTON MARTIN

CHAMPIONSHIP WINS: FOUR

Driving for **Red Bull,** Vettel became the **youngest** ever **F1 World Champion** in 2010 and went on to take the title another three times in a row, with Hamilton finishing no higher than fourth. Lewis won their closely fought battles in **2017** and **2018** and says that the rivalry with Vettel was **"his favourite"**.

LEGEND

NAME: MICHAEL SCHUMACHER

YEARS IN F1: 1991-2006, 2010-12

TEAMS: JORDAN, BENETTON, FERRARI, MERCEDES

CHAMPIONSHIP WINS: SEVEN

Schumacher, like Hamilton, did not have the wealthy background of many F1 drivers. Starting racing in a **go-kart** built by his **dad,** he went on to win the F1 World Championship **SEVEN** times, a record equalled only by Hamilton. The F1 legend was tragically injured in a skiing accident in 2013.

LEGEND

NAME: **ALAIN PROST**

YEARS IN F1: **1980-91, 1993**

TEAMS: **McLAREN, RENAULT, FERRARI, WILLIAMS**

CHAMPIONSHIP WINS: **FOUR**

Prost was famous for his careful, **"scientific"** style of racing – very different from the intense, aggressive style of his great rival **Ayrton Senna.** The French F1 legend is one of the all-time greats and another of Hamilton's heroes.

LEGEND

NAME: *JUAN MANUEL FANGIO*

YEARS IN F1: *1950-51, 1953-58*

TEAMS: *ALFA ROMEO, MASERATI, MERCEDES, FERRARI*

CHAMPIONSHIP WINS: *FIVE*

Fangio was the man to beat when Formula One began in the **1950s.** His win record of **24** out of **52 races** remains the highest and only Hamilton and Schumacher have won more F1 Championships than Fangio. Hamilton calls him the **"Godfather of our sport".**

RIVAL

NAME: *NICO ROSBERG*

YEARS IN F1: *2006-16*

TEAMS: *WILLIAMS, MERCEDES*

CHAMPIONSHIP WINS: *ONE*

Rosberg and Hamilton's **karting** rivalry moved to F1 when they were **Mercedes team-mates.** Rosberg's precise driving style and **quiet personality** was very different to Lewis and the two regularly **clashed** on and off the track. Their rivalry pushed each other as Mercedes dominated F1.

NAME: **NIKI LAUDA**

YEARS IN F1: **1971-79, 1982-85**

TEAMS: **MARCH, BRM, FERRARI, BRABHAM, McLAREN**

CHAMPIONSHIP WINS: **THREE**

The **1975** World Champion, Lauda was severely burned after a crash in the following season. Incredibly, he missed only two races and was **champion** again in **1977.** One of the greatest ever F1 racers, Lauda, who became a mentor to Lewis at Mercedes, is the only driver to have won the title with **Ferrari** and **McLaren.**

LEGEND

James Hunt was - like Hamilton - a bit of an **outsider** in F1. Starting out with the "amateur" **Hesketh Racing,** Hunt was **wild** and **aggressive** on the track and frowned upon by the authorities. His close friendship and rivalry with **Niki Lauda** was tested when he won the **1976** Championship after Lauda's crash.

LEGEND

NAME: *SIR JACKIE STEWART*

YEARS IN F1: *1965-73*

TEAMS: *BRM, MATRA, MARCH, TYRRELL*

CHAMPIONSHIP WINS: *THREE*

With a rock star image, Stewart was an early **F1 celebrity.** In the late **1960s** and **70s**, the **'Flying Scot'** was the driver to beat. His ideas about media, sponsorship and safety in F1 were revolutionary and with **THREE** World Championship wins, he is the second most-successful British driver.

RIVAL

NAME: *MAX VERSTAPPEN*

YEARS IN F1: ***2015-***

TEAMS: ***TORO ROSSO, RED BULL***

CHAMPIONSHIP WINS: ***ONE***

In 2015, aged just **17,** Max Verstappen became the **youngest-ever** F1 driver and the following year, in Spain, the **youngest race winner. 'Mad Max'** drives without fear and has turned early mistakes into winning form. His **2021** World Championship win over Hamilton could be the first step to **F1 greatness.**

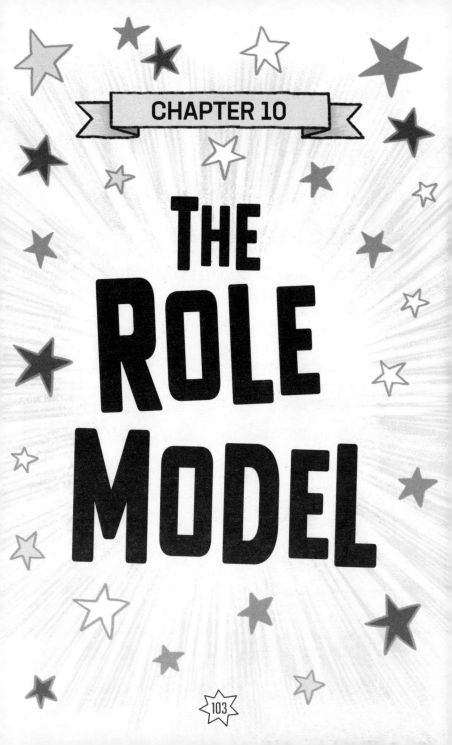

CHAPTER 10

THE ROLE MODEL

Hamilton is a **world-beating F1 champion** that few others can match.

He has used his unique position as a **person of colour** in one of the world's most exclusive sports to speak out against **racism,** inequality and other issues.

"BEING THE FIRST BLACK 'ANYTHING' IS A PROUD AND LONELY WALK."

During the **2020 season**, Lewis said his activism inspired him to his **seventh** World Championship.

Lewis is an **inspiration** to young people of all backgrounds. His success in motorsport shows that anyone could become a **driver** . . . or **engineer** . . . or **technician.**

Lewis has also campaigned for

environmental issues around the world . . .

"I FLY A LOT LESS NOW. I'M TRYING TO FLY LESS THROUGH THE YEAR . . ."

Lewis sold his private jet in 2019.

Animal rights . . .

THANKS LEWIS!

Lewis has been vegan since 2017.

And launched **Mission 44,** a charity to improve education and employment opportunities for young people from underrepresented groups.

"I EXPERIENCED FIRST-HAND HOW COMING FROM AN UNDERREPRESENTED BACKGROUND CAN AFFECT YOUR FUTURE . . ."

M44

HAMILTON IS AMONG A NUMBER OF BLACK SPORTS STARS TO MAKE A STAND.

JESSE OWENS
ATHLETE

At the **1936 Berlin Olympic Games,** black US athlete Jesse Owens won **FOUR GOLD MEDALS,** embarrassing Germany's evil Nazi government.

ARTHUR ASHE
TENNIS PLAYER

Ashe is the only black male winner of the

Australian Open, the **US Open** and **Wimbledon.** He fought for the rights of black people in the **USA** and **South Africa.**

MUHAMMAD ALI
BOXER

Known as **'The Greatest'**, Ali is one of history's biggest sporting icons. In the 1960s, he was an outspoken opponent to the **Vietnam War.**

ALTHEA GIBSON
TENNIS PLAYER

In the 1950s, Gibson was one of the top female tennis players. She was the first black woman to win a **Grand Slam** event and went on to win **four** more.

"WE HAVE TO KEEP STRIVING FOR EQUALITY FOR ALL, IN ORDER TO CONTINUE TO SEE TRUE CHANGE AND LASTING CHANGE IN OUR WORLD."

Lewis Hamilton

CHAPTER 11

HAMILTON RULES

Hamilton also has ambitions to get into music. In 2020, he secretly sang on a **Christina Aguilera** track under the name **XDNA.**

An F1 driver worth **£225 MILLION** will have some cool cars, right? **Correct!**

Lewis has an **AWESOME** collection including a . . .

MERCEDES AMG-ONE

VAROOM!

£1.7 MILLION

Lewis became **SIR** Lewis Hamilton in 2021, when he was **knighted** for his services to motorsport.

Lewis is the fourth knighted Grand Prix star after **Sir Jack Brabham, Sir Stirling Moss** and **Sir Jackie Stewart.**

Sir Jack Brabham

Sir Stirling Moss

Sir Jackie Stewart

RACING RECORDS

Lewis Hamilton's racing record book is nothing short of astonishing. Here are some of the big ones:

MOST F1 WINS
103

MOST F1 POINTS
4165.5

MOST POLE POSITIONS
103

MOST PODIUM FINISHES
182

TOTAL LAPS LED
5396

TOTAL RACES LEADING EVERY LAP
23

TOTAL POLE AND WINS IN THE SAME RACE
61

Lewis is the **only driver** to win a race in every season he has finished.

HONOURS AND AWARDS

F1 WORLD DRIVERS' CHAMPIONSHIP

2007
2014
2015
2017
2018
2019
2020

F1 WORLD CONSTRUCTORS' CHAMPIONSHIP

2014
2015
2016
2017
2018
2019
2020
2021

FASTEST LAP AWARD

2010*	2017
2021*	2019
2014	2020
2015	

* = shared

POLE POSITION AWARD

2007*   2016
2008   2017
2009*   2018
2012   2020
2015

* = shared

BBC SPORTS
PERSONALITY
OF THE YEAR
2014
2020

FIA PERSONALITY
OF THE YEAR
2014
2018
2020
2021

QUIZ TIME!

How much do you know about **LEWIS HAMILTON?** Try this quiz to find out, then test your friends!

1. Where was Lewis born?

---

2. How old was Lewis when he began racing karts?

---

3. Who was his team-mate in Formula A karting?

---

4. How many Grand Prix did Hamilton win in his debut season?

---

5. Which driver did Lewis narrowly beat to win his first Championship?

---

6. Which German driver was his big rival from 2009 to 2014?

----

7. How many times has he won the British Grand Prix?

----

8. At which Grand Prix did Lewis lose the 2021 Championship to Max Verstappen?

----

9. Which famous F1 city is Hamilton's home?

----

10. Lewis secretly sang on a track by which pop star?

The answers are on the next page *but no peeking!*

ANSWERS

1. Stevenage, England
2. Eight
3. Nico Rosberg
4. Four
5. Felipe Massa
6. Sebastian Vettel
7. Eight
8. Abu Dhabi
9. Monaco
10. Christina Aguilera

F1 WORDS
YOU SHOULD KNOW

Pole position
First place on the starting grid.

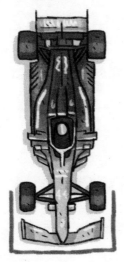

Podium finish
First, second or third place at the end of the race.

Constructors' Championship
The Formula One team competition. Each team enters two cars in a race.

Safety car
Car that comes on the track to slow drivers down if there is an accident or another problem.

HAVE YOU READ ANY OF THESE OTHER BOOKS FROM THE SUPERSTARS SERIES?

SPORTS SUPERSTARS

MORE COMING SOON!

FOOTBALL SUPERSTARS

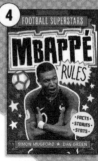

ABOUT THE AUTHORS

Simon's first job was at the Science Museum, making paper aeroplanes and blowing bubbles big enough for your dad to stand in. Since then he's written lots of books about everything from dinosaurs and rockets, to BMX bikes, football and motorsport. He lives in Kent with his wife and daughter, a dog, two tortoises and a cat.

Dan has drawn silly pictures since he could hold a crayon. Then he grew up and started making books about stuff like people's jobs, football, big machines, space, *Doctor Who* and *Star Wars*. He lives in Suffolk with his wife, son, daughter and a dog that takes him for very long walks.